Tracks I've Left in the Snow

by
Frank Howard Hall

Compiled by
Nettie Hall

HALL'S SLEDS
5875 Mc Crum Road
Jackson, MI 49201

First Published by Halls Sleds 3/31/2008

ISBN: 978-0-615-20172-6

Printed in the United States of America
Chelsea, Michigan

This book is printed on acid-free paper.

Preface by Tim Karasek, a young friend of mine for many years. He helped me make sleds, he rand dogs for us, he went hunting with me, an he made a home from the same pine planting where I got mine 25 years before he did.

Acknowledgements:
Thank you to Carrie Hair and Melissa Obrinske for helping me put Frank's book together. I could not have done it without their help.

Contents

Preface

It is often said that occasionally, when the stars and the planets align just right, extraordinary things have the potential to happen. I am certain that was the case the day I met Frank Hall.

As a younger man I had been recently reassigned to be Assistant Manager at a branch of a bank in which Frank was a customer. On a particularly frigid morning, Frank walked in. A man with a walk of a particular purpose, wearing a worn Carhartt jacket and a fox fur hat with a leather brim. Aside from his hat, he stood out from everyone else, a warm smile, a quick wit, a joke and a quiet self-confidence that drew others toward him. I could tell by brief inspection that he knew nothing of "male day spas", "metro-sexuals" or designer fashion. He came from a different era. A time when being an outdoorsman was not just for sport, but for necessity, a self made man whose success was built on doing what he loved. Whether out of a curiosity of nature, the love of a good story or the need to fill some unknowing void in my life, I knew that I had to meet him.

I introduced myself and we immediately struck up a conversation on Alaska or sled dogs or some other fascinating topic for a city boy such as myself. Each time he came to the bank I would make certain I said "hello", if only to see if I could coax yet another story from him. Eventually, Frank would invite me to visit his home, an invitation to which I would eagerly accept.

When I first pulled up to the address that I had written down on the bank deposit slip, I was pleasantly surprised to find a log home with several outbuildings on a sizable piece of land. Being a fledgling hunter, I was immediately impressed with the layout and hoped that some of the "trappings" normally associated with such living would be found inside. Driving past the kennels containing some 50 dogs, I was greeted by Frank who emerged from the sled shop. With a smile on his face he invited me in for a cup of coffee because it was time for a break. Passing the threshold, I immediately felt like the child in the candy shop, immersed in the warmth of the wood and the stone while taking a mental inventory of the array of mounted animals decorating the rooms, each signifying a particular life experience for Frank. We would sit and talk for hours, an event which would repeat itself countless times over the next 25 years of friendship. Regardless of where life would take me in the years to com, college, marriage, or to work in the western woods, I could always depend on returning home to the oak table oasis where the coffee was always hot and the comforting conversation began where it left off, days or weeks before.

I could say beyond question that the topic which dominated many of our discussions revolved around firearms, hunting, sled dogs or anything related to the outdoors. Some of my greatest memories a field are from hunting woodchucks or whitetails in Frank's back yard or elk and antelope in the western states to driving the back-up team of sled dogs for Frank and his wonderful wife Nettie. He was a particular pleasure around the campfire and always had the uncanny ability to inject a story, joke or poem at just the precise time to generate a laugh or to see the humor in any situation. It is with deep regret that the stories that come to you on the following pages do so posthumously, as Frank has moved on to hunt more prosperous grounds with friends past. But, these are some of the same wonderful stories I have had the pleasure to hear countless times, each with a slightly different twist. It would please him for you to enjoy them every bit as much as I have, for they are a tribute to Frank Hall, friend, husband, father, hunter, and master sled-builder.

Enjoy!

Tim Karasek

My First Tracks

Over the years a lot of people have said to me "Why don't you jot down the story of your life?" I've thought long and hard about it and have jotted down a few chapters and have decided it's going to be quite a chore writing down things I have experienced. It's a lot harder than sitting over a cup of coffee and telling it. I have had quite a few tales to tell and maybe a few people would be kind enough to read them. I doubt if it would be a best seller but I have decided to give it a try.

Over the years I have read people's stories and in print it didn't sound like the person who wrote them at all. Hopefully this won't be like that. I hope what I put in print does sound like this old duffer.

I'm not much on flash backs so I'll start from the beginning. I want to start off a little different by saying I have a big sled loaded and a strong team just waiting for me to pull the snow hooks. I don't want to be accused of talking to myself so I want to take you in my sled and start down the trail of my life. We've got good snow and a packed trail and if we run into bad weather I've got a cabin we can hunker down in and provisions in the sled so we'll probably be ok. SO you jump in my sled, pull that big blanket over you and we'll be on our way. We'll meet a few people on the trail that has been a big part of my life so we'll stay and chat with them as we meet them along the way. So here goes, so hang on tight and we're off.

The first people we'll stop and chat with are my parents. What they wouldn't have time to tell you, I can fill in as we go down the trail. My dad was from Indiana. He knew a lot about steam engines. In his early days he ran a steam thrashing machine for a farmer. He was working on a dredge boat in the low country digging canals in Kentucky. And that's where they met and married. My sister came before me then I came along. Both of us were red heads along with my mother. My brother came along 5 years after me.

This is something I thought amusing. I was just up off the floor and talking. Anything that I was afraid of I'd say boo before describing it such as Boo Cow or Boo man. On one occasion we were walking down toward my grandmother's barn to see a new calf that her cow had in the barnyard. I was trotting ahead of my mother and Granny and maybe my sister. They told me not to go too far ahead, I might step on a boo snake. So I was the first to the barnyard and barn and that cow stuck her head around the corner of the barn and said, "MOOOO." I just about turned inside out. I ran back to the group scared to death and said that boo cow scared me. They all got a chuckle out of that.

As a Youngun!

A big thing in those days was once a week a huckster would come by with household things in a wagon pulled by horses. He'd have bells so we could hear him coming. We'd head for the henhouse and grab an egg and run out. When he stopped, we would trade him an egg for bubblegum. It was a great day! I was barefooted and freckled.

We didn't have electricity. We had coal oil lamps and water from a spring up the road. We had no refrigeration so most of the meat was pork which you could preserve by salting and hickory smoking. Everybody had a smoke house off to one side of the yard. Smoked ham or bacon was a big part of our diet. Sliced bread was unheard of. So every morning, my grandmother, who we called Granny, would get a fire going in the kitchen range and bake biscuits for breakfast.

The only automobile I'd see in a day would be the mail carrier. Our mode of travel was horse and wagon. If we went to town a couple miles away, we had a hitching rail in front of the stores. The railroad ran parallel to Front Street. When a train was coming into town, the engineer would blow the whistle and everybody who had horses tied to the hitching rail would make a beeline to hold the horses. It was too scary and you'd have a runaway when the train came into town. Life was serious but there were humorous moments.

When I was 4 or 5 years old, my dad had a chance to come to Michigan and work for a power company. This is when my brother came along. He's still my baby brother but he's bigger than me. So Jackson, Michigan was our new home. It's where I started kindergarten. We had a modern little home in the eastern part of town. A freeway goes by there now. Things were going pretty good for awhile. Then the great depression hit. My folks lost the home and then my dad had a gallbladder removed. This was before medical insurance. So they went to a finance company to pay the medical bill which was $1,500. My mother took us kids and went back to Kentucky to live with my grandmother. My dad stayed in Michigan where he had work.

We lived a couple years down there until my dad was transferred up to Newago, Michigan, to take care of a big storage yard with all the equipment that built the earthen dam on the Muskegon River, which was called Hardy Dam. It was late summer of that year before school began. This was on a railroad siding off the Pere Marquette RR at the end of a two track.

A Foreman's house was lifted on a flatcar by a big crane at the hardy dam site and set off to one side of the siding. It was 24 ft. x 24 ft. My dad later added a front and back porch with 3 wood burning stoves. The back porch became the kitchen-- no plumbing, no electricity. It added up to 5 rooms and a path. This was going to be our home for the next 6 years. My dad was paid a salary, which wasn't an awful lot, especially after the monthly payment to the finance company for his gallbladder medical bills which came first.

We lived close to nature. Rabbits and fish were a big help. We finally got a couple cows for milk and butter and butchered a couple pigs in the fall and with a good garden, we survived. Now all this was before snow tires, chainsaws, and 4 wheel drives.

So life was pretty simple. As a kid I didn't know the difference. Your TV, Pizza, McDonalds etc weren't around. You don't miss something you never had. The Sunday comics were a big event. I'd like to say my parents were very wholesome people. They believed in the golden rule and I felt we were brought up in a good wholesome atmosphere. My father was very stern. When he spoke to you, you listened. He had a great ability handling big equipment and figuring things out. This is where I learned or developed my ability of seeing something done and figuring out how I could do it.

My mother was the salt of the earth. Both our parents

neglected themselves for us kids. There was no other way to do it, and both very honest persons.

When I was 12 years old we discovered a growth on my leg. My boots wouldn't close up. My mother checked my leg and found the growth. They operated on it during one of the hottest times of July, 1936. The doctors were afraid they would have to cut some important tendons in my leg and if they did, I'd never be able to walk on it again.

They stretched it enough but when I was in the hospital, I thought I might not ever be able to walk. One day a nurse gave me a magazine to look at and on the cover was this picture of snowshoe tracks going into the distance. It gave me the inspiration to make a lot of tracks in the snow.

A picture similar to this that I saw in July 1936 gave me inspiration to make a lot of tracks in the snow when it was doubtful I ever could. 2-87 Frank Hall

While in high school in Sparta, Michigan, I ran 4 years in track--holding a record for the 100 yd. event that held for 11 years. I also played on the football team and did pretty good.

1941 Running the Mile in High School

When in high school I made my first sled. The shop teacher showed a bunch of us how to steam wood. I made a pair of skis, a toboggan, and a dog sled.

Using My First Sled and My First Dog

My Little Brother in My first Sled

The Load of Wood for Which I was Using My First Sled

I had never been to a library and the village library was a block from the high school. I got to spending noon hours in the library reading about the North Country. That's when I got acquainted with the books written by James Oliver Curwood and Jack London. I couldn't wait to read one book after another.

They were about the Northwest Mounted Police chasing an outlaw in the winter by dog team or going down a river in the wilderness in a canoe. All of these topics were right up my alley. Years later, I started collecting books of interest to me. I collected all the Curwood titles. Most are collector books today and out-of-print.

In the ninth grade literature class, I gave a book report for extra credit on a Curwood title. I thought I was doing a good job. The teacher was a first year teacher just out of college. At the end of my oral report she says I could spend my time better than reading Curwood. I bristled up on this remark and I said, "For instance, what?"

Steinbeck's Grapes of Wrath had been recently published and she said that would be a good place to start. I looked her in the eye and said, "I'll stick with Curwood!"

One summer back in the 50's I got talked into selling stainless steel cookware. I didn't get rich but it was an education. It was a good product. I'm still sold on it. I sold around home but often I'd head north to different towns. An incident at Gaylord is worth telling. I called one afternoon on the mother of a friend. It was a bright August day. We sat in the backyard at a picnic table under a big umbrella. She was a nice, middle aged lady. I had some time to kill so I stopped. We had chatted 10 or 15 minutes and she said to me, "I bet you have an interesting horoscope." I was at that time going through a real domestic problem and reading my horoscope was the last thing I wanted to hear about. I was having a hard time handling one day at a time—let alone the future.

So I said, "I'd rather not!" and related to her what I've already said.

Anyway about every 10 minutes, she would say, "I'd like to read your horoscope."

Each time she said this, it was harder to say no. After about the 5th time she said this, I said , "There is only one way that I'll let you do it. You have been talking to me for almost an hour or so. You have learned a bit about my personality so if you can tell me within one day of my birthday, I'll let you."

She said, "No problem! Your birthday is April 10th." My birthday is April 9th. This was almost spooky!

I don't remember anything that disturbed me so after awhile, I went on my way. But she did tell me something that I shrugged off but remembered.

She said, "By the time you are 56 years old, you're going to be dealing in a product that women like."

Some years after I was making sleds full time, I was sitting in church and my mind was wandering. It came to me of what this lady had said. Still to this day I sell more sleds to gals than guys. This is hard to believe but it's true. My reply to that is, "Wonders never cease!"

SLEDS

My first view of sleds was big freight sled pictures. I had seen them in articles which were in magazines once in a great while. In those days the racing sled was another breed of cats. They had long extensions in back. This truly surprised me. I got to thinking a light racing sled would be similar to a pair of skis. You'd stand almost in the middle because if you stand on the rear of the runner you'd sink in the snow and that would have the sled going up hill all the time instead of using the floating feature of a level runner on top of the snow. A big freight sled doesn't need big long extensions because the sled is longer and the weight is going to keep it somewhat on a level surface. Ed Moody from New England was the only source of sleds at that time.

My first sled was made out of hickory saplings that would bend green and it was a long sled I used to haul things in like stove wood, etc. My second sled was made after I got to high school and learned how to bend wood. It was a far cry from the style I ended up developing later. But I had to start somewhere. The use of the sled determines its style.

I don't remember for sure the first real sled I saw. I think it was in Sparta. I fellow I know had it.

Time went by until about 1959 or 60, the sport of running sled dogs came to the mid-west making sleds in demand. The fellow I had lent my sled to decided to make a couple of sleds and I got to thinking maybe I'd make sleds some day. He borrowed a 6 inch hand planer and his only other tool was a jack knife. Well, he made a sled and wanted me to take a look at it. I stopped at his place and looked the sled over. He asked me what I thought of it. The style wasn't too bad but he was determined not to use any bolts or screws, just pins and rawhide. As I was looking it over I said, "Wouldn't it be a lot more simple to put a bolt or screw here or there?"

He stiffened up and said, "They'd never sell!" He was

pretty set in his ways.

I said I was going to make sleds someday and I'd be using bolts and screws-as well as rawhide. He was the kind of guy who would go hungry before he would change his mind.

By that time the sport was catching on and they needed sleds. I had been a body man working on wrecked cars and trucks for quite some time. Things were slow in the shop.

A little race was coming up in a week or so. I got permission to take some time off work. I went to a sawmill and got some raw lumber, borrowed a table saw and jointer from a friend and set up shop in my mother's garage. I'd learned how to bend wood in shop in high school so in a week I whittled out 6 sleds of different sizes. I didn't have a pick up truck so I put car top carriers on top of my car and tied the sleds up there. I headed to the race. I had $2.00 in my pocket. All six sleds sold by noon and I had orders for more. I came home with $242.00 in my wallet. I guess this put me in the sled business making sleds which have become Hall's Sleds-known world wide.

By this time I had gone through a nasty divorce and my second wife, Nettie, wanted to relocate. We picked Jackson, Michigan. Nettie was a school teacher and at first we lived in a mobile home in a trailer park for a few months. After a while we saw 12 acres for sale and ended up buying it with adjacent land available to use.

Our first priority was to have a dog kennel and trails to run the dogs. We had the trailer moved to the property and had to have a well put down. We were really counting pennies. I got a job in a body shop so we were on our way. Nettie was for all the plans we were making and our first building was a kennel building.

Before buying the 12 acres I had gone to the township and made sure I could have a kennel. So we leveled a spot, set the footings for a kennel building, and put it up out of cement blocks. I bought some old lumber for the roof. We didn't have

Practice run on our 12 acres of land. Silver,
Umiak, Tanny and Stormy. I'm training for
the Jackson, Michigan race in 1963

funds for new nails so we pulled nails and straightened nails and spikes and put the roof on it. I made a door and put in a wood stove. We were crowded but this was my first sled shop. We added on to it later. That gave us more needed room.

I picked up tools and machines that I needed: table saw, jointer, drill press, hand drills and such needed to make sleds. I bought white ash lumber at a sawmill-rough sawed and I fabricated the lumber to the size I needed for sleds. In order to have straight grained lumber, I had to sort the good stuff. I had to have it good enough to use especially good wood for bending the front bows and handle bars which had to be good straight grained lumber.

By this time I had developed my own sled design. A sled has to be tough and strong to take the rigors of abuse on the trail. I didn't want to copy any other style or design. I wanted it to be a Hall Sled.

I had skied several years and in order to change directions and steer where you're going, you bend your knees sideways and in doing so the skis go on edge which gives with the up sweep of the front of the ski and enables you to turn on skis. I came up with stanchions which are the uprights coming up from the runners and cross members with a bolt holding them with a proper designed handle bar. The sled could be maneuvered like skis. I called it a swivel sled. You can steer the sled in going around curves on the trail by leaning on the inside of the turn and the sled would naturally lean that way. Thus the runners would be somewhat on edge. This is one of the greatest ideas in sled building. In fact, I paid to have it searched out in the patent office in Washington, DC. It had been patented several times but not on a dog sled. My patent lawyer said my idea was so simple that it might not be able to be patented and he advised me to get it on the market and the idea would probably be safe. He was right. It has taken over 35 years for it to catch on. But all the European sleds have all the cables and pulleys to make their sled do what mine does so simply. To hear them tell about it, it was just invented but this old duffer on McCrum Rd. outside of Jackson, Michigan beat them by over 30 years.

Most sleds that are made today are made to flex in this manner.

Some are even made with a separated handlebar so they can flex especially those used on the Iditarod in Alaska.

I grew up looking at wood so I was blessed with the

knowledge what good wood was all about. Here in the Midwest, we have the luxury of having good wood available. My idea of a sled is to use good straight grained wood. A lot of sleds are made by laminating the pieces and gluing them together. There are a couple reasons they do that. They can use a lower grade of material plus they don't know how to bend by steaming or boiling. They can bend these layers of wood and glue it in a form for parts of the sled that have to be curved.

I've never laminated because I use good wood and bending has never been a problem. Plus I've never trusted glue all that much. I think using full strength wood is the traditional way of making a sled. The traditional sled was made by a person that had sled dogs and he needed a sled. So he made a sled using materials available. I think the sleds I make comes pretty close to being what I consider how a traditional sled was made. I use bolts, screws and rawhide. I think I am the only sled maker that still uses rawhide. Rawhide is hard to find and is messy to make.

Scribing a Log

Using the Peavey to Turn a Log

Setting a Log

Peeling Logs by the Front Door

Our Log Home

Our Log Cabin in the Beautiful Snow of '82

Building our Front Porch

Notching a Log

The New Front Porch

*Tim Karasek's home made from the same pine
planting as mine, only 25 years later*

*Our Shop before the Fire.
The sled in this picture is a sled that was made by
German prisoners of war in World War II. It is now in
the Michigan Whitetail Hall of Fame Museum. There is
a display of several of my things there.*

Our New Shop after the Fire

There are several features my sleds have. On the racing sled, my front bow is long enough to go all the way back to the rear stanchions. The middle board of the bed goes all the way forward to be connected to the front bow. My rear bow or handle bar slants forward. I form a tripod on the angle to the rear of the front and back stanchion thus crossing the front bow making a double triangle. This is the strongest possible way for two pieces of wood to be fastened together. While we're talking about handle bar or rear bow, my rear bow is not part of the two side upper rails; they are separate. Some sleds are made with upper rails and handle bars all one piece. They look nice but are impossible to flex and a sled has to flex going over an uneven trail.

There are a lot of good ideas that have improved features of sleds. I was having breakfast with Charlie Boulding a couple of years ago. He came up with a statement that I couldn't have said it any better myself. We were talking dogs, equipment, etc, that some of these ideas that come up are good even if you didn't come up with them yourself. The QCR (quick change runners) was a great idea that Tim White came up with. The aluminum bar brake was a great idea. I came up with a snow hook holder with a safety feature that keeps the snow hook from coming out should you take a spill. This is a good safety feature because if you spill and are being drug down the trail with a snowhook bouncing near your face, it is a dangerous situation.

Cutting up slats. Runners are on the form. Upper rails are behind me. Stantion sets are in the back room ready for other sleds.

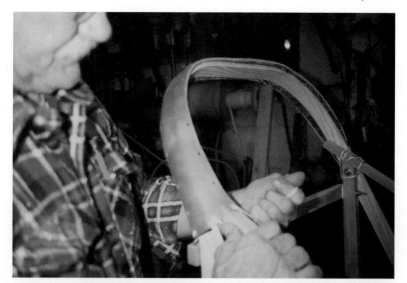

Tieing the Rawhide on the Back Bow.

Getting a bunch of sleds ready in the summer.
They'll all be gone by Christmas.

Another thing that's been a problem over the years is a tread to stand on. This is on top of the runners, where you stand while going down the trail. Snow builds up where you stand, making it hard to stay on the runners. I think a lot of things have been tried-some good and some not so good. There are some made out of special rubber that are quite popular. I, by accident, came up with the most simple. It's a static mat used in front of a desk for a desk chair to roll around on above the carpet. It's plastic, smooth on top, but has little bumps on the bottom side that press down into the carpet so it doesn't move around. This cut into two inch strips, eighteen to twenty inches long, with the bumps up, put on top of the runner with five screws really does the job quite well. Snow doesn't stick to it and your foot doesn't slide off.

Working inside our very first shop.
We were very crowded.

At the Iditarod banquet some years ago, I took a few sets and had them with me. My table was next to Martin Buser's so

Martin picked up a pair and said, "These are for me, aren't they?"

I told him, "Yes, but why are you so interested in them?" I had sent him a set the year before and the set ended up on the sled that went to Nome in first place. He won the race.

He said, "Frank, this is the greatest idea that ever hit Alaska. They get a little brittle at 60 below. A lot of things would get brittle at 60 below."

I didn't tell him what they were made from but it finally caught on as to what they were made from. Most every sled maker is using the mat cut in strips at this writing.

In the sled business to date, and in our sport, we have to come up with things already in existence that we can apply to be used in our needs.

In our new shop when we were the busiest in our business.
Allison Scott and Dave Robison helped Nettie and me.

Weight has been a big factor in ideas about sleds. There's only about 10 lbs. difference between a light sled and a heavy sled. I've had guys who wanted a sled that if they could throw it up in the air on a breezy day, it would land 30 feet downwind.

That's impossible. I've worked with wood about as much as anyone and sixteen lbs. is minimum for a good sled. By the time you get plastic on the runners, bar brake attached, snowhook and holder added, you're talking 25 to 28 lbs. They could loose 10 to 15 lbs. off their fat tummy. That would be easier. The bottom line is, it takes a certain amount of wood to have a certain amount of strength. Sure, I could make a 10 pound sled out of an orange crate, but it wouldn't make it around the first curve—let alone back to the finish line.

There are sleds made today that have no wood in them at all but they still weigh a certain amount. In most cases good wood is not all that easy to find.

My 5000ᵗʰ Sled

As of today I have made over 5000 sleds and am crowding upwards of 6000. No other sled maker has come close. My 5000ᵗʰ sled is in Owosso, Michigan, at the Curwood headquarters there. In fact I labeled the sled the Curwood model, named after James Oliver Curwood, the famous author who wrote several books about the North. I got acquainted with his books in high school and fell in love with his titles along with Jack London.

The second day of 1999, I had the misfortune of loosing my shop by fire. My neighbor, Mike Howard, was helping me butcher a cow for meat for the dogs when the shop caught fire near the 100amp fuse box. I hollered to Mike to turn off the shop power downstairs while I shut off the fuel oil tank. The phones were dead so Mike ran across the road and called the fire department.

The big fire truck came in but then backed out again. I thought he was going for more water but actually it was a pin missing from the PTO that runs the main pump. He had to go to the hardware store and get that pin. By the time he came back, the shop was in really bad shape. I think 4 or 5 fire trucks came, including the rescue truck, etc.

Our Shop after the Fire

This was one the real bad days of my life. The heart of most of my activities was gone. I thought some things might be salvageable. The walls were still standing but the roof was caved in. I got the big bolt nippers and cut the end of service wires and telephone wires and duck taped them up. Then the phone worked.

I called the motel where Nettie was staying for a race in the UP. Finally the fire was out and the smoke cleared away. I was numb and was for a long time.

Soon the snow was coming down heavily. I put our horses in early. It was almost blizzard conditions. I fed the critters and came in the house. I had many phone calls. Nettie returned my call. When I told her the shop had burned down, she didn't say anything for a long time. It's hard to describe the emotional thoughts and feelings when something so horrible happens. There were some pluses. Nobody got hurt. It happened while I was here in the daytime. Most everything can be replaced.

It took us awhile to regroup. We thought about going back in our old little shop but we had replacement insurance. We rebuilt and we were out of business only three months. I retooled and to date have as modern an equipment as available.

I'll never get rich at what I do but there's a great satisfaction in it. It changes people's ideas about winter. They are able to have an affordable sled, a couple dogs that they already have to pull them around. It shortens the winter and youngsters in most cases really go for it. It keeps them off the streets and it's better to be influenced by a pet then otherwise. Who knows! They might become a world figure in our sport.

One of the comments I often make is, "I work hard when I work; I play hard when I play; and I rest hard when I rest!" I'm pretty well known for what I do.

I have made quite a few big sleds to be used to take people on rides at Lodges and such plus Iditarod sleds that take a real beating. My flexible sled was proven on the Iditarod. I sponsored a fellow in 1986 by making a four stanchion sled for him. He had leased a team from Joe Redington to train and condition for the race. Halfway to Nome, he was leading so Nettie said, "You'd better get to Nome." So I ended up in Nome for the finish. He had slipped back a ways in the race. But he did quite well for a rooky. Susan Butcher won her first time and my good friend, Rick Swanson, took third.

You're allowed three sleds to run the race in case of a wreck. In fact Terry Atkins was on his fourth sled when he came in. But the guy that I had sponsored had just one sled and it was mine. He made it all the way to Nome. It was one of the first sleds to do that- to make it all the way to the finish line. Several drivers wanted to look at the sled that had make it to Nome all in one piece. I do make a tough sled but the secret is that they flex. I was real proud.

In fact several of my sleds are in the race every year. To date, I have been at the start 10 to 12 times. So I am pretty well known up there. I've been to the finish line twice. In August of 1962, I started running an ad in the classified section of the Alaska magazine that has run for over 42 years. That's got to be a record. I'm proud of the fact that I have sleds all over the globe.

GLSDA, ISDRA,MUSH

Alaska was the heart of sled dog racing and still is. But by the 1960's, there were 3 areas in the lower 48 that were developing into sled dog worlds.

New England was the most organized. There was a small group in California and then a growing group of races in the mid-west.

Teams were starting to go from one area to another and found that some racing clubs had rules that were unfamiliar to the traveling team. There was a developing need for a standard set of rules and therefore in 1966, a group from the various areas met in Niagara Falls, NY, and formed the International Sled Dog Racing Association or ISDRA. Some of the well-known and somewhat famous in the sled dog world attended. All were aware of the need for standardized rules across the racing world. Some mushers who attended were Jean Bryar (women's world champion), Dr. Lombard (a famous world champion, who by this time raced mostly in Alaska and was many times against world class competition) and MacDougal (famous Canadian racer).

We started by recognizing all present. I brought a copy of GLSDA's (Great Lakes Sled Dog Association), constitution and race rules. It was used as a guideline.

We divided into committees and I worked on the races rules committee. GLSDA's race rules were used as a starting point and we went on from there.

I had the honor to work with Dr. Lombard who was a vet from Massachusetts. We worked all weekend (early morning until late at night). By Sunday P.M., we had ISDRA with standardized race rules off the ground and in print. Any wording could be updated in future meetings when it seemed necessary and fitting. But it was a start.

To date, some 45 years later, changes have been made: wording and new ideas or needs. It is a working organization which has become internationally known.

New clubs forming have access to a proven constitution and bylaws instead of the hassle of coming up with one themselves.

Today, wherever you race, you know what the rules are. Almost all top races in the world are ISDRA sanctioned which means that not only will we run by ISDRA rules, but also they are evaluated by ISDRA. Forty some years ago we met to standardize the sled dog world. I feel we succeeded.

Nettie and I became charter members and I was a director for many years. One year I was secretary. I'm proud that Nettie and I were pioneers of ISDRA and felt our time well-spent for a worthy cause.

In the late 1970's, there developed a need in Michigan to have two clubs. GLSDA ran for purse and was closely associated with ISDRA (we always sanctioned our races with ISDRA and always had a purse).

A new club called Mid-Union Sled Haulers (MUSH) was formed. They could not-by their constitution-have a purse.

They were a good group. They were into camping out over the weekend and although they were competitive, it was more important to enjoy each other than to compete against the best teams in the country.

There was also a group of mid-distance drivers who were quite competitive. Some of them ran and usually finished the Iditarod (a 1200 mile race from Anchorage to Nome).

We always supported these other groups with advertising and such but GLSDA was our home club. Nettie, being a teacher, was quite organized and therefore was often the president or some other office in GLSDA.

***Don and Alice Hall and Nettie and me. This
was taken the evening of our wedding
April 12, 1962***

***I'm chatting with Cousin Barb during a
family get-together***

Nettie and I, daughter Laura and her friend.
We went on a cruise together in 1984.

KALKASKA

The Great Lakes Sled Dog Association was growing and I felt that we needed a big annual race—one to be proud of having. So I looked the Michigan map over and talked to a few people. One was a fellow who worked for the Department of Natural Resources (DNR). We needed to zero in on a good snow belt with lots of state land. So I picked Kalkaska which sort of fitted these conditions.

I went up to Kalkaska and introduced myself to a few people, letting them in on what I had in mind. One of the persons I talked to was a business man who owned a snowmobile dealership whose name was Carl Leach. I also went to the Chamber of Commerce and talked to them. All these persons thought this was a great idea because at that time Kalkaska had a population of 1300 and needed a shot in the arm.

Nettie and Me and Carl Leach (our great supporter on making Kalkaska a great race).

Now this was before snowmobiles much. There were a number of people in town who formed a snowmobile club and had a clubhouse on the western part of town at the edge of a vast state land area. This was before there was any idea of groomed trails, etc.

The snowmobile people drove 'two tracks' and such here and there and knew the country like the back of their hand. They were all for having a sled dog race. They were also the means for packing the trails for a race. The name of the club was the Snow Packers Club.

By this time I felt I had picked the right town for the race. This was late 1964 so by early 1965, we had the makings of a place to have a sled dog race. Lavon Barve was a lot of help that year. He later moved to Alaska and won a lot of fame in the Iditarod-the big long distance race from Anchorage to Nome—1200 miles—which had gained world renown

Well, by this time things were looking up for getting an established winter event in Kalkaska. We came up with a small purse. The Snow Packers packed the trail and we had our first race in Kalkaska with mainly mushers from our own sled dog club but not many out-of-state mushers. The snow packers became trail help where it was needed.

The first race went well enough so we started planning for the following year. We corrected the few problems that had come up.

There are several things to consider when putting on a well-planned race. You have to have (1) snow, (2) trail, (3) parking, and (4) purse. You can go on and on but these are the main things needed.

Kalkaska has been a big part of my life and as of this writing Kalkaska is the second longest existing race in the lower 48–forty years makes Laconia, NH number 1.

A short few years, we used two tracts for trails-packed by our friends with their snowmobiles. Then the state saw fit to establish groomed trails for the snowmobile crowd and we could train on them. On the race weekend we could use the portion of the groomed trails which proved to be like a freeway. The traveling mushers labeled Kalkaska's trail the best south of Fairbanks, AK.

As Kalkaska grew, we became a major race in the lower 48. I even won it a time or two before the world champions started coming. Even then I improved also. One year 29 teams entered the unlimited class. We drew our own starting positions that year. I drew # 26. I was devastated. I had a great team and that meant I had a lot of passing to do. Our trail was 17.8 miles. I ended up passing 10 or 12 teams and was 22 seconds out of first place. This wasn't too bad for a corn fed country boy. That meant that the second day I'd go out #2. I had an equally good run the second day. I held my position so I ended up second for the race which was pretty good as 2 or 3 of the drivers had been world champions. I was real happy ending up in second place. It was the highlight in my racing career. Harris Dunlap took first place.

I should mention our parking method at Kalkaska at that time. It was the best. The lanes for parking all headed toward the starting chute and, in a herringbone fashion angling toward the starting chute, a slot was plowed for the vehicles to back in. This made it super. Most drivers were very satisfied.

Over the years by improving the methods and such, Kalkaska grew to be a very successful race. We had the best trails, parking was good, and we had good snow. Our biggest problem was coming up with a good purse. All this time, Kalkaska was growing by leaps and bounds. Oil wells were being drilled all over. In fact, on several occasions, I had to change the trail especially in the unlimited class. Big oil rigs and loads of pipe were the norm on the highways. The population grew so fast that the schools had early and late classes.

Things went like this for several years and, of course,

snowmobiling exploded. The big, fast machines became popular. They were killing themselves—35-40 a year in Michigan alone. So for safety sake, we had to give up racing on the groomed trails. Quite a change came about. The big unlimited teams started fading. It was up to us to make a separate set of trails for dog racing just to be safe.

I said to the DNR, "Show us where on still existing adjacent state land that we can make trails and we'll cut the trail."

So a number of us got together with axes, chainsaws, and such and came up with a new set of trails starting at the fairgrounds. We ended up with 4 dog, 6 dog, and 8 dog trails having a common start and finish. There was no head-on passing and had a right hand cut off for the 4 and 6 dog courses. Unlimited by that time was almost nonexistent in our area but

Tom Edge and me by one of my big sleds. Tom and I spent all day out on the Kalkaska Trail putting up markers. When other people took over this job when we got older, it only took them a couple hours. They say we spent too much time visiting our stashes along the trail!

we came up with circling the western loop twice and came up with mileage enough to include unlimited in our schedule. I feel good about Jason Rodenhouse. He kept the unlimited alive so we have ended up including that division on our agenda.

So Kalkaska is alive and well at this writing. Of course, they still have growing pains being handled as they come up.

I was the race chairman for a lot of years. My job now is to see that the trail is ready for the race day. Marking the trail is important. With Tom Edge, I feel we do a good job. Over the years I've received a lot of credit concerning Kalkaska but without the help of all the volunteers, I seriously couldn't have done it alone. Some have passed on like Carl Leach who was a great help in the early days. Tom and Mary Guy, Chuck Hill, Tim Kimball, Rick and Margaret Harvey, George and Darci Lewis, Hal and Mary Dufford just to name a few. My wife, Nettie, did a super job of figuring out parking and a lot of little details.

In talking about the race and ideas some time back, I came up with and voiced an idea which took form. We have a junior class. Why not have a senior class? Anybody over 60 with a few gray hairs, etc. could run. The reply was, "Do you have to be that old?"

I said, "With gray hairs and a cane, I guess we could lower the age."

So it has taken on as an enthusiastic class at Kalkaska. I even won it the first year. It was my last race. Nettie won it once. But it has added a lot of fun for the older guys and gals

.Another thing I might mention are the great rigs that people drive now days. The big new shiny trucks and the rigs for the dogs are a real sight on race days with all their rigs in their spots. Dogs are picketed around the vehicles with dogs barking and people talking on the P.A. system. It all sounds like a lot of confusion to a spectator but there is a plan to it all.

My last race. I won the Senior Classic in 1995.

Senior Classic in 1995
Hal Dufford, Marve Smith, Tom Edge, Frank Hall

On Sunday, after all are gone, and silence has taken over the grounds, there's a realm of sadness that it will be another year before this will all happen again.

An interesting feature about Kalkaska is in 40 years, it has been cancelled only once. Kalkaska grew to the extent that over 180 teams would enter the contest which made it the biggest race on the globe. We're proud and solving needs that arose that have attracted so many teams with comments that it's the best race of the year.

ELY

By the late 60s and 70s other races developed besides Laconia. The other two that come to mind that drew world class drivers was Ely, Minnesota and Kalkaska, Michigan. I ran the first year that Ely had a race and did fair but one of the things I remember well was Saturday morning it was 50 degrees below zero

By 1970 I had developed quite a string of dogs. My training trail at home was farmer's fields with not 200 feet of level ground. It was all up hill and down. I often said I just kept adding two more dogs until the hills didn't bother me much. This developed a super strong team. I almost never had an injured dog. They muscled up and then got stronger and faster.

The summer of 1969 a young fellow pulled into my yard with a Ford Mustang pulling a trailer with 5 or 6 dogs of all descriptions one being a big Siberian and some others the guys in Minnesota had given him as a joke. His name was Mike Murfin. He wanted to run dogs and learn all he could. He turned out to be an all A student.

He was here a few days and one cool morning I said, "You know, we could run a team of dogs."

He went ballistic. I had a rig that 2 people could ride on so we harnessed up and headed out. It was just a small team so we'd have to run up the hills. We got back and Mike had a pair of oxfords on his feet with no socks and he had blisters on both heels and he was so excited, he didn't even notice it until later. He was hooked!

He had come to Michigan through Wisconsin and stopped at a couple kennels along the way that were about half friendly. Anyway, he ended up on McCrum Rd. here in Jackson. But he had a problem. He had a wife back in Minnesota who was calling a couple times a day.

My advice was to go get his wife, get a place to stay in

**Getting around the trails to check on teams
before ATV's**

town with his wife and get a job and after work we'd train dogs
and see what we could come up with. So he did. We fixed him
up with dog houses and a corner of my kennel fenced in area.
He got a job, a dirty, hot job in a foundry through a friend of
mine. His wife got a job also.

That fall, when nights cooled off, we ran 4 or 5 teams.

We picked a dog out of his gang that would lead and he picked up a couple more and came up with a seven dog team. My wife Nettie and I were running unlimited (10-14 dog teams). Another fellow, a beginning driver named Dean Bishop, ran our lesser dogs that hadn't made Nettie's or my team. Our kennel boy ran a 3 dog team. We had a going outfit.

That fall our club had a training weekend in a western Michigan forest area with a good trail. We took 42 dogs altogether. We ran a measured trail and were timed. I took first and Nettie took fourth in unlimited. Mike took first and Dean took second in 7 dog class. Our kennel boy took first in 3 dog. We weren't very popular. It proved what training could do.

We kept on training hard for the upcoming race season. The tougher you can train the better. Then if you run into bad trail conditions, it would be a piece of cake. We don't get early snow this far south in Michigan and most often we'd go north to run on sleds during the holidays. This also let the dog stretch out on flat country. We ended up doing quite well in the races we entered but the race we had our sights on was Ely, Minnesota.

While training here at home, quite often I'd pick a spot where I could watch the teams go by. Sometimes a sharp eye can see things that the driver behind the team doesn't see. Along in January, we got snow enough to run on sleds. I went out on the trail to watch Mike's dogs go by. Through concentrated training with these supposed misfit dogs that had been given to Mike back in Minnesota last summer were shaping up pretty darn good. After the run, I said to Mike, "If when we go to Ely and your dogs run like they did today, there will be some eyebrows raised." This is what we trained for. My dogs were doing super as well. So the weekend of Ely was approaching and we headed for Northern Minnesota.

I had called Lew Wheeler who I got my first dog from. He lived at Crane Lake, Minnesota. He was a bush pilot at this time. It was Friday before the race on Saturday. We were parked on the designated place on the street. I saw this plane circle and

Lew Wheeler and I at his home around 2000

land on a lake at the edge of town. After awhile a little guy with snowshoes over his shoulder came up the sidewalk. He got to my truck and asked if Frank Hall was around. Well, I hadn't seen Lew for several years. It was great that he flew down to Ely to see me. Just at that moment, Dick Moulton and Geo. Eslinger were coming from the other direction and low and behold Lew and these two guys were in the K9 Corps during WWII and hadn't seen each other since the army days. It was a back slapping reunion. Lew and I chatted for awhile and went our separate ways.

That evening at the driver's meeting, our starting positions were predrawn and my number was 6. I looked over the names and I figured I'd be leading the race after a short time. This came true.

The next morning it was 47 degrees below zero. By race time we had a heat wave of 35 degrees below, I just cringed because the race course was down plowed roads, across lakes, and at that temperature, trail help might be late. We were taking dogs out of the truck. Mike and I and quite a few people were looking my dogs over. I guess the word was out that I had been doing quite well. One fellow from Quebec, a Frenchman who talked broken English, looked my dogs over and said, "Your dags run goot?" That was amusing to me. I answered that they had been running quite well.

The race began and I left the chute and as I figured, I passed the early teams in short order and was tooling down a plowed road and was coming up to a T. No trail help in sight! I was on the left side of the road and had to make a right turn. My leader started left, I put the brake on and slammed the front of

Ely, 1967 Nanook (40 lbs) in lead
Randy and Slick (65 lbs.) at point

the sled in the snow bank. I made my way up to the front of the team and swung them around to the right. I had a couple dogs hopelessly tangled and going backwards. I went this way for about ¼ of a mile. I couldn't stop but up a ways was trail help that turned us off the plowed road, through a meadow to a lake. Well, I got untangled and went on my way without any more trouble but that cost me first place. There were about 30 teams entered so second place wasn't too shabby.

Then it was Mike's turn in the 7 dog race. I don't remember any problems he might have had but he came in first. All weekend he had a crowd of followers wanting to know how he did it. He'd point to me, and said, "Go ask the professor." He called me 'The Professor' He often said I was John Wayne without a camera in front of me. Anyway we sure showed those guys who were sort of making fun of Mike with his mangy bunch of dogs that were pawned off on him. We drove back to Michigan elated.

Telling the people at Ely what I thought of their race

This was the first race Ely put on. Saturday night there was a nice banquet and all were having a great time with speeches by different people. Merv Hilpiper was one. At that time I was a director of ISDRA (International Sled Dog Race Association) and was asked to say a few words. The question came up as how was the race going, etc. I'll never forget what I said.

"From what I've seen today, you guys are on your way!" The roof nearly came off the banquet hall and it was the truth. There were many great races at Ely in the following years with world class competition.

LACONIA

There came a time I had won most every race in Michigan so I decided to hit a big race and run with the big boys. I picked Laconia, New Hampshire, the World Derby. I was greeted with all the fan fair. I had driven further than any other entry to the race. I was hustled to a couple radio stations to be interviewed. This was really big time! Dom Blodgett from Maine, who ran Coon Hounds, was there also.

There were three things I wanted to do. Number one was not to get disqualified for some unknown reason that I might not be aware of. Number two was to represent our Great Lakes Club as I was the first person from the Midwest to enter the race. And third was I wanted to be a good sport and learn as much as possible.

I met some to the big names who treated me as their equal. World Champion Jean Bryar, Dr. Belford, and Dick and Cindy Molburg, editors of Team and Trail, a monthly publication in our sport are some examples. A fellow by the name of Benoit took me under his wing. Actually I had a dog that had been his. He knew the race course like the back of his hand and proceeded to take me around by car to show me some of the little spots where I might have trouble. By the time he got done with showing me all of these little spots which amounted to quite a number, I felt like I should have stayed in Michigan.

This was my first three day race.

There were 30 entries in the race. Masses of humanity were at the starting line which was downtown Laconia. Friday morning came and butterflies were flitting in my stomach. Our starting positions were drawn and I was #5 so the countdown came and I was on my way. We went out through town, down streets to the edge of town then into the rolling countryside, road crossings and such. It started to snow. It snowed 13 inches that day. There were a couple places on the race course that the outgoing team met the incoming teams. That meant meeting a team head-on which I had never done before. I entered a meadow and looked up. Here came a big team and behind him another, then another. Three teams came all at once. I was running 12 dogs and they went on the right hand side of the trail and no sweat. I was real proud of this first encounter of meetings teams head-on.

In the course of the race I could hear hounds baying. Then it dawned on me that it was Dom Blodgett with his team of Walker Coon Hounds. I felt like the fox that was trying to stay ahead of them. Actually they were the fastest team on four legs. Well, I completed the first day back in the pack. I felt great but I had really gotten up a sweat. All the road crossings and such were manned by former dog mushers. If you needed help-approaching a crossing, all you had to do was put an arm up and wave it. That meant you wanted them to grab your sled so you could make an adjustment someplace in the team. They really

1966, third day at Laconia. Nanook and Boots in lead.

knew how to help. The first day of the race went pretty well.

The second day, of all things, I went out number one. There was an event I'll never forget what happened that day. I hadn't been passed by a team as yet and had crossed roads and got by the halfway part of the trail across a meadow. I was approaching a side road and a snow plow had just plowed the road which left a five foot wall of snow where the trail crossed the road. My heart came up in my mouth. My leaders hit the middle of the road and vaulted up the five foot wall on the other side instead of going one way or the other down the road. I was overjoyed with my leaders. Of course, they knew the trail from the day before. A little further on, I heard a guy holler, "Trail." He said it loud enough so there was no question as to what he meant! I thought I was tooling along pretty good across the meadow. It was Charlie Belford. He went by me like I was tied to a tree. This is the most helpless feeling a guy can have. In another minute, Charlie had disappeared.

In the parking area, getting ready to harness my team, I could hardly move for people wanting to see my sled that swiveled. No one had ever seen one before. In fact, a familiar face I'd seen pictures of was in the crowd, smoking his pipe. It was Ed Moody, a famous sled maker from New England. He looked my sled all over and I'll never forget what he had to say. "Frank, you do good work. Before you're done, there are going to be a lot of these around." I don't know about his prophecy but he couldn't have said it any better because to date, I've made over 5000 sleds.

Well, I finished the three day race. The third day I went out number seven. I didn't have to drop a dog. I met a lot of people on that trip and I learned a lot. I accomplished what I went for. It was a hurdle in my life as a dog driver.

Ed Moody at his home just chatting

In my early memories, sled dogs gave me a thrill I still have. Working behind a team on a trail of snow in front of a sled with a driver in back and in the background are evergreens with their tops pointing sharply toward the sky and a log cabin in the foreground gives me a thrill that I can't explain other than I'm thrilled through and through!

As I look back over nearly a half a century mushing dogs and being around and acquainted with mushers—some my competitors and most just friends—a lot with similar goals mostly wanting to do better each year as the seasons come. A lot of get-to-gethers were just to learn from each other as different subjects that came up that were pertinent to the sport. I have noticed over the years that nobody knows all the answers and nobody is unbeatable. I give a lot of credit to the musher who year after year comes up hard to beat. Your dogs get older and have to be replaced plus training conditions change from year to year. Once you get to the top, you are the target! Over the years, on a tough race, I'd rather be a few seconds in second place because the guy in first place isn't going to sleep good that night. I've experienced both sides of this situation!

One of the things that is part of becoming a wise musher is seeing trouble developing before it happens and to nip it in the bud. Believe me, from the back of the sled, it's amazing what your trained eye can see. A very disturbing thing is having a person who is supposed to be trail help stand beside an event happening, watching it, and not making a move until it's too late. This is when patience becomes stretched.

IDITAROD

My first trip to the Iditarod was in 1980. A fellow from Milwaukee, Wisconsin, went also. We flew up to Anchorage and stayed with Lavon Barve in Wasilla. He lent us a truck and we visited several kennels.

Lavon picked us up at the airport. He's a printer by trade and on our way out of Anchorage, he dropped off articles he had printed at different locations. On our way we stopped for a bite to eat and I had my first of many bacon burgers, a super sized sandwich.

We had tickets for the banquet on Thursday night. It was quite an affair! During the evening, the mushers drew their starting positions. Of course, it was exciting! I met and saw a lot of big names.

During the afternoon before the banquet, I was sitting in the big hotel lounge watching people coming and going—Joe Redington, Rick Swenson, etc. Rick had won the Iditarod a couple times already and where he went there was a crowd following him around. The driver's meeting was going on upstairs for mushers only. On one occasion the elevator door opened so I turned to see who was there. It was Rick Swenson. He stepped out and stopped to look around. He walked right over to me and said, "Frank, I've been wanting to meet you." Well, it made my day. I said it was great to meet him also. We passed the time and he went on his way being followed by several people. Anytime Rick would say anything, it was like that EF Hutton commercial on TV. Every thing went silent.

The banquet went great and we headed back to Lavon's for the night. The next day was Friday so we visited several kennels. Iditarod musher's attitude just about blew my mind. It was the day before the start of the 1200 mile race. One musher said I've got to check at Medley's harness shop to see if my harnesses are ready. Joe Redington said I have got to see if my sled is ready over at Olsons. This was the norm of the day. Last minute stuff which I thought was getting pretty late. But this was their way. Ted, the fellow who was with me, and I shrugged our shoulders in disbelief.

We visited one kennel and looking the dogs over, I said to Ted, "There's not a dog here that isn't half wolf." The musher got home and verified what I had said. It was this team that he had gone to Nome with them a year or two earlier.

We didn't go to the start on Saturday. Lavon said it was a huge traffic jam but we would go to the restart later in the afternoon. It was at Nancy Lake, west of Wasilla. It was a great event seeing the dog teams leaving the starting chute, heading down a road for a mile or two, and then heading into the wilderness. There was mass humanity on each side of the road as far as you could see.

I had a chance to chat with Rick Swenson for a few minutes. I wished him well and he was on his way with a 20 dog team. What a sight! He looked very qualified to be doing his thing. What a day!

Lavon Barve and me on 4ᵗʰ Ave.

The next day, Sunday, Ted and I chartered a flight with a bush pilot to fly us out to Skwenta, about three check points out on the trail. We landed on the river. Some teams were already there. This was about a hundred miles from Nancy Lake, the start of the race the afternoon before. They had made good time.

The flight in the bush plane was exciting, flying up the rivers with the trail down below and teams stretched out on the trail some a mile apart, others 3 or 4 miles ahead. It was a great sight! All my life I'd wanted to go to Alaska and this was my first time. It was exciting.

At Skwenta, we got out after the plane landed. There were a few teams resting on the river. I walked over to the chief checker. He checks the arrival time in and the departure time out. I was curious as to how many teams had already left. Joe looked and his chart and counted eight. Then he says to me, "Did you just get off a plane?"

I said, "Yes." He wanted to know who I was so I told him.

He said, "FRANK HALL!!!"

He hollered over to the other checker and said, "You do this. I have to show Frank around." So he introduced me as we went. He walked up the snow stairway up the river bank to his log cabin. A couple caches on 4 legs were in his yard.

We went to his back door that had strips of bear skin around the door to keep the cold air out. He says, "Look who I brought in!" The cabin was full of people who I was introduced to.

One was a young fellow who was holding a youngster. I said, "Did you deliver him yourself?"

He said, "Yes." Life is different in the bush of Alaska, you rise to the occasion.

The reason Joe was so taken by my visit, he had gotten a sled from me a couple years before. His daughter and another girl were going down the trail with a small team and were charged by a moose. The little gal riding in the sled got hit in the head with a horn and hoof and was in a coma for a few days. She finally came around but the sled got damaged pretty bad. In Joe's, I was treated with cookies and coffee. It was a great time! Joe said, "It's like Grand Central Station around here today." Everyone was having a great time.

I went back down on the river and at that time Rick Swenson was parking his team over to our side. I went down to chat with Rick for a few minutes. I took a compass off my cap and I said to Rick, "Do me a favor and take this to Nome." He said OK and gave me a pair of fuzzy gloves in a sandwich bag with a book of matches included in it. I still have them unused.

We flew back to Wasilla and in a day or so back to Wisconsin and Michigan. It was a very memorable trip-a time to remember.

Six years went by. During that time Libby Riddles and Dean Osmar had won the race to Nome. Libby was the first gal to win it.

In late 1985, a young fellow from up near Petoskey, Michigan, came down and wondered if I'd sponsor him with a sled to run in the Iditarod. I agreed. I made him a four stanchion Iditarod sled to be used in the 1986 event. He had leased a team from Joe Redington, Sr. and during the race was doing quite well. He was doing so well he was leading the race about half way through it. My wife, Nettie, says to me, "You'd better get to Nome and welcome him in." So I decided to go. I flew into Anchorage, stayed a night, and then headed for Nome on another flight. A lot of excitement was in the air. I stayed at the radio station.

I might say right here that Nome is not the heartbeat of America. The race is the biggest thing that happens in Nome in the year. The station was buzzing. It was reporting the progress of the race. Front Street is the finish line where a team goes under the arch of the big burls. At the arch there were masses of humanity cheering.

I got there a couple days ahead of the finish so I could absorb a lot of things. I spent a lot of time at the Iditarod headquarters getting acquainted with whomever. I was delighted to meet and spend a lot of time with Leo Swenson, Rick's dad. I knew Rick was from Minnesota and in the course of chatting, I asked Leo how Rick got started wanting to run dogs and such.

He said they owned a farm in Minnesota and the year that Rick graduated from high school, Leo leased out the farm. So Rick headed up into the northern part of the state and got a job at a large lake where they rented out boats and motors to fishermen. Rick's job was to guide fishermen as to where to fish and such. There was a fellow who was a bush pilot that flew fishermen up into Canada to fish. Rick got acquainted with him. He had been in Alaska in the mid 30s. He had had sled dogs and ran a trap line there in winter before becoming a pilot. He and Rick spent a lot of time together talking dogs and such. It became a desire of Rick's to some day run dogs. This fellow told him that if he wanted to learn how to run dogs and get good dogs, he'd have to go to Alaska. My name came up quite often.

While Leo was telling me this, I asked Leo, "What was the fellow's name who Rick got acquainted with?" He tried to tell me but couldn't remember the fellow's name.

I asked, "It wasn't Lew Wheeler, was it?"

He said, "Yes!" Of all things it was the same fellow who low these many years ago I had got my first dog from. This was unbelievable. No wonder Rick came across the hotel lobby in 1980 to see what this guy looked like that Lew had mentioned so often.

A lot of people fly into Nome for the finish of the race. The tallest building in Nome is 3 stories tall. Everything that gets to Nome is by boat in summer and by air in the winter. Milk is $6 a gallon. Cows are pretty scarce! I hear that the Burger

King there is one of the chains biggest outlets. It wasn't there in 1986.

When a musher in the race gets within a mile of the finish, a siren blows. Everything stops. The whole town heads for the finish line. Even school lets out kids, grabbing boots and coats, and heading for Front Street and the finish!

Susan Butcher, back in '86, came in around midnight. It was her first win of four. People came out of the woodwork even at that time of the night. People were crowding each other to get as close as possible to the fence. There was cheering and lots of noise. Joe Gurnie, 2nd place, was back in Safety resting along with Rick Swensen who was back a ways. Joe came in about an hour after Susan. He was the local favorite. He was a native Alaskan. It would be a while before Rick would come in so most people went back to bed.

The next morning, just at daylight, Rick crossed the finish line. Of course, the siren went off and everybody headed to Front Street. I was standing in back of a bunch of school kids and after the cameras and a lot of questions which took about 10 minutes or so, Rick asked the kids, "Aren't you supposed to be in school?"

Then Rick saw me standing back of some students and said, "Hi, Frank! Your compass is on my sled." It was 6 years before that I had given the compass to him.

It was quite a day! Other mushers came in from time to time. Rick put his dogs in a truck and headed for a quiet place for a well deserved rest. He needed to get some sleep! The last couple hundred miles of the Iditarod, the drivers don't get much sleep. They do get a short few hours at White Mountain, the mandatory rest stop heading to Nome. This is 77 miles and then they dash for the finish line. They have to stay awake.

The next day after Rick finished, he came down to the Iditarod headquarters. The governor of Alaska, Robert Sheffield was there. I was introduced to him as a big sled maker from the lower 48. Other important people came in. Burt Baumarff , president of the Iditarod Trail Committee at the time, introduced me to the governor.

After things settled down, I walked over to Rick and said, "I had no idea you knew Lew Wheeler."

He said he learned how to trap beaver from Lew and that they spent a lot of time together that fall. My name had come up quite often. He said he knew something about me that I didn't know. He went on to tell me my dad had detested the fact that I'd bought a dog with money that could have been used a better way. Times were hard then and it had caused a problem in our household that I wasn't aware of. Rick said my mother wrote Lew and asked him to never sell me another dog because it caused so much trouble. Of course, I didn't know this until then. My dad didn't live to see what that dog Bella, my first dog, and my making sleds had done in my life. I'm sure he would have been quite proud of my accomplishments because of it. My mother was very proud. She lived long enough to see some of what I had done.

I left Nome after getting more acquainted with Rick. We had a kindred spirit going. This was a good feeling. A little trapper from northern Minnesota gave 2 guys a start that has made quite an impact on the mushing world to date. He, I'm sure, was very proud of this. He passed away in 2005 at the age of 94. Anyway, it was a thrill to spend some time with Rick and to get to know him somewhat at the headquarters in Nome.

I had tickets for the big final banquet. We saw up to that time, the biggest purse passed out to the first 20 places of the race--$300,000. The lad that I sponsored with the sled came in about the middle of the pack. Most mushers have at least 3 sleds for the race. They have a couple at different check points to be used in case of a wreck. Mike, the fellow who I sponsored, had just one sled that left Anchorage with it and made it all the way to Nome-which maybe was the first sled ever to make it all the way. Several of the mushers had to look at it. As I mentioned earlier, Terry Atkins was on his 4th sled when he crossed the finish line. I talked to him later about it. His first sled gave out and he bought a new sled at a check point from a native. It didn't make it to the next check point. The sled that he finished the race was a damaged sled Rick Swenson loaned him so he could finish the race. All the sleds take a beating. I was proud that my sled had made it to Nome in all one piece.

My trip to Nome was quite an event. In fact, I started going to the Iditarod at least every other year for the next few years.

I became acquainted with Joe at the Eagle Dog Food Company which I'll go into more detail later. We became good friends. For several years, I went with a group from the Eagle Dog Food Co. We had great times together. Joe and I introduced members of our group to the big names in the race. Joe sponsored a couple big names in the race.

Well, I have gone many times. I always had a great time. As I mentioned, I went with the Eagle crowd several times. Then I got acquainted with a group from Owosso, Michigan—namely Ivan Conger and Denny Vogel. One year I made a sled for the Iditarod for a fellow who had moved to Alaska from Michigan. His name was Kris Swanquarin. He ended up becoming the rookie of the year coming in 20th place with my sled. That year this group from Owosso including myself made 10 people went to the Iditarod together. I might mention Owosso was the home of the James Oliver Curwood, the famous author of many northern titles and Ivan is the top authority on the life of this famous author. Incidentally, he was my favorite author, also.

There was a big celebration in early June each year in Owosso of James Oliver Curwood. They had a big parade and such that year. I had made a one of kind sled (it was my 5000th sled). It was a wooden toboggan style sled. Ivan saw it and was curious as to what I was going to name it. I got to thinking of the name of the 'Curwood Model.' The idea went over big. The fellow who was from Michigan who became the Rookie of the year in the Iditarod had come down from Alaska to visit his mother. All these things came together The Owosso gang thought a float would be nice to enter the parade with my Curwood sled, the chap and his wife from Alaska, my wife, Nettie, and me. We had a nice float designed. It was a huge event with over 2 miles of floats. Low and behold, we took the top attraction float of the parade. Ivan was beside himself so I decided to contribute the 5000th sled to the Curwood headquarters building to have on display with a big plaque, with a dedication ceremony and all the fan fare. What a weekend!

At the Curwood Days Parade our Float took 1st Place for Most Interesting

The next year or so, Denny cut a big white ash tree with the idea that the wood would go on an Iditarod sled for P. Kisser, who needed an Iditarod sled. I built it with all the fan fair included.

My latest trip to the Iditarod was with Joe from Eagle

Dog Food. Just he and I went on the trip. Joe made all the arrangements on where to stay, etc. We didn't go to the start but to Nome for the finish. Martin Buser, who is sponsored by Eagle Dog Food, won. I had a chance to spend some time with Rick Swenson again. Martin became an US citizen at the finish which was a big event with all of us waving a little US flag and singing the anthem. Just at the close of the ceremony, Al Hardman from Michigan crossed the finish line. Col. Vaughn was there along with most of the community of Nome. What an event! Martin is from Switzerland. This was his fourth win.

The next morning, before heading back to Anchorage in route to Fairbanks, we had breakfast with Charlie Boulding and his wife. Charlie is a delight to talk to with his long white beard and the twinkle in his eye. Joe and I really enjoyed breakfast with him and his wife at Fat Freddies Restaurant on Front Street.

Something interesting came about that first year the Owosso group went to the Iditarod. There were 10 of us. We rented a big van to haul 10 people. It was the day after the banquet on Friday. We drove to Wasilla and went to the Iditarod headquarters- a big log cabin-and then down the Knik Highway to Joe Redington's home. I got out and went to the door. Joe and Vi greeted me and I said I had some friends with me. Joe says, "Bring them in." This was my greeting- the same at Martin Busers. Then all of a sudden I realized I'm a tour guide and I guess I was without really knowing it.

We stayed at a motel near the Anchorage Iditarod Headquarters at the Regal Hotel. The other way down the street was Gwinnies Restaurant. It was a quiet place to eat. Grits and salt pork were on the menu. Gwinnies is a must as a part of the Iditarod trip. It's rustic with an upstairs as a great place to go eat and see a lot of interesting people. It's considered an Old Alaskan Restaurant.

I guess at this writing I have gone to the Iditarod 10 or 12 times. I'm pretty well known among the musher's crowd. I've had lots of sleds in the race most every year.

Another thing I'm proud of is in August of 1962, I started running a small ad in the classified section of the Alaska Magazine on dog sleds. I ran it continuously for 44 years. It's probably a record.

The Iditarod is an exciting event every year with the ceremonies starting in Anchorage. They haul in snow on 4th Ave the night before the race so they have snow on the streets until they get to the edge of town and hit the trail to Eagle River, the first check point.

The dog trucks are parked in accordance with their starting position. I for several years got an official arm patch to help mushers to the starting line. It's pretty tough going 2 or 4 blocks holding on to that sled or a couple dogs in 8 inches of

Joe Redington Sr. (father of the Iditarod) Edgar Nollner (One of the dog drivers who took the diphtheria serum to Nome) and me (just a spectator at the Iditarod)

hauled in snow. It is pretty tiring like walking in a bowl of sugar. The teams get lined up 3 or 4 waiting their starting time with a lot of noisy people and of course the PA system announcing who is in the chute and the count down. Then the teams are on their way to Nome 1200 miles away. If you helped a team in the chute, you step aside to make room for the next team. Most often around 80 teams head out to Nome. All in all, it's been great fun. I'm glad I've been part of it.

In the early days a driver could start with a 20 dog team but in recent years they have cut back to 16 and make just as good a time and, of course, they have 4 less dogs to care for. I do love the sight of those big teams. That's Dog Mushing!

Martin Buser while visiting his kennel on Friday before the race.

Libby Riddles (first woman to win the Iditarod, 1965, visiting our shop, Joe Cocquyt (of Eagle Dog Food) and me. This picture was taken around 1996)

Dogs

I have had quite a few dogs that have made a difference in my mushing career. There's an old saying that in a man's lifetime he should have one good dog, one good watch and one good wife. As most of you know, Nettie's my wife and has been a big part of my mushing life. She has picked up the loose ends, I probably could not have done what I have done without her. That covers the wife. Now for a watch! I have had several, some better than others. They seem to last only so long. They are pretty easy to replace. Now for the dogs.

By now I have mentioned my first sled dog, Bella, from Lew Wheeler. This was quite an event in my young life. It started a life time of events. She was 8 months old when I got her. She was very wolfish. Lou later told me he was trying to figure out who the father was. He finally came to the conclusion it was a wolf. He lived in northern Minnesota so this was quite possible.

There was an interesting event the day Bella arrived in Sparta. She came by train from Minnesota. I was in the eighth grade in a country, one-roomed school. It was the afternoon of Sept 28, 1938. I remember it well. The door of the school opened and it was my mother with a distressed look on her face. She got permission to take me from school which was granted. On the way to the car she said my dog arrived in Sparta in a crate and at the depot was put on a flat bed truck. On the way to the freight building, the dog chewed out of the crate and was running loose in town. My heart sank. Someone had driven out from town to tell my mother this. On the way to town, which was 5 miles, I'll never forget what my mother said to me. "We've got to catch that dog even if we get chewed up doing it."

We got to town and were told where the dog was. She was laying in a shady yard and people were standing at a distance watching to see what was going to take place. The truck driver was there with a pound of hamburger waiting for me. Of course, being from the back woods of northern Minnesota and not being around crowds, she was going to be pretty shy. I was handed the hamburger and proceeded to do my best to get her by the collar. She was full grown and weighed at least 75 lbs. so I was being as cautious as I possibly could be. Very slowly I made my way toward Bella, calling her by name and making no quick moves. In a few minutes I was petting her head and slowly got her collar in my hand. She was mine and a lot of spectators were relieved including the truck driver who felt quite responsible for her well being. She rode home in the car with a very happy kid. All I could think of up to the moment that I got her by the collar was working all summer raising an acre of potatoes for my $15.00 share to the crop. That's the story of the arrival of my first dog, Bella. Times were really hard. I had to figure a way to make enough money that summer to pay for the dog.

I got a pretty fair lead dog from a guy in New York State. His name was Smokey. He was a fair trail leader but not a command lead dog.

I got a little Siberian from a fellow in Canada. Nanook came from well built ancestors. At least he could stay in front of a whole team of pretty fast Alaskans. He had to keep from getting run over at Ely, Minnesota. He ran out of gas the last day about a quarter of a mile from the finish line and my 2 big point dogs pushed him across the finish line. I have a picture of that finish. He had run out of gas so you couldn't even see him at the finish. He was hidden behind the point dogs.

It's a luxury to have 2 or 3 leaders in the team in case one has trouble or gets injured.

I got a half lab from Ann Wing in New York State. She got him from George Attla. He was like driving a bicycle. His name was Darky. He had a habit that he played on anybody putting him in the dog box. You had to push him up about shoulder high to put him the compartment, head first. Before you could close the compartment door, he'd turn around so quick with his head sticking out go, "ARFF! ARFF! ARFF!," You wouldn't expect this. I'm sure he wouldn't bite, but it sure woke you up. Once in a while, when someone offered to help put the dogs away, I'd say they could put that dark dog in his compartment that said Darky. Then I'd stand there and watch the fun. As you closed the door, he'd settle back in the compartment with a satisfied look on his face that he'd done his duty for the day.

Darky was a valentine's present for Nettie. She ran Darky and her regular double lead, Comet, in lead the day we got him in the Kalkaska race. This was something that we never did. We always checked a dog out before putting him in lead in a race. We did it and it turned out super. The two dogs worked together to perfection. When we got him home, Nettie spent the summer getting Darky ready to run lead for her the next year.Darky would do nothing right. He had been trained by Attla and we

Ely, 1970, I took 2ⁿᵈ. Jerry Riley took first. Here I'm coming across the finish line. Nanook, the lead, was so tired the point dogs (Slick and Randy) needed to help him finish.

knew he had been chain trained but she refused to even show a chain to Darky. Finally she became completely frustrated and decided to use the chain. She tapped him very gently on the nose with the chain and from that day on, Darky was a perfect lead dog. As a matter of fact, he became so perfect he was moved up to double lead in my team and ran there for several years. When I retired him, I gave him to a mid-distance friend who loved Darky so much he became his best dog he ever had--friend and lead.

I ran a dog by the name of Boots. Beside Nanook, they made a good set of leaders. After she no longer could run lead in my team, Nettie took her over. She was a perfect single lead for her. She tells of one race that she ran in Grand Haven, MI. It was a one day race. They started down town and moved out to the shore of Lake Michigan, did a turn around and came back the same trail. This meant running a rather shy single lead by all kinds of spectators, cars, and other teams. Boots ran a perfect race and Nettie claims that despite the fact she came in second, it was the best race she ever ran. The next day she ran a fun race in the wilderness. She ran the unlimited race just for the fun of it. She had run only in the 7 dog class before. Boots did everything wrong. She ran up on the top of the side of the road instead of down on the smooth running trail and then turned around and literally laughed at Nettie. She still ended up winning the race (Of course I and the other top competitors were out of state competing) but Nettie said it was one of her fun races because there was the fun communications between her and Boots.

She came from Alaska but as the years went by, our good leaders we trained ourselves. If you have one good leader, it's lot easier to train another leader-especially if you can set up a good trail system to work on commands

Nanook and Boots—The two best leaders I had
Nanook –a reg. Sib. From Canada
Boots-originally from Alaska through Jean Bryar and Walt
Barnhart to me.

You never want to let the leader make up his own mind on a decision or a choice of Y trails. If he wants to take the left trail say, "No! Gee" and vise versa. They learn quite fast. This keeps them on their toes when a decision comes up. In recent years, we've had 5 or 6 good command leaders. You can never have too many leaders.

Training with an ATV is great. If your leaders take the wrong turn, you can stop, back up, and make them go the way you want them to go. You can't do this with rigs. One of the best leaders we've had was Carmack. He was a big 65 or 70 lb. leggy, blue eyed, lightning fast, a real joy. It was real hard to find dogs in our kennel to compete with him. He died at 6 years old, suddenly, with no forewarning. It was a real sad day at our home. Frosty was a great leader for us. He's getting older now and we don't ask him to stay up with our younger speed merchants.

Carmack

Another special dog was a little dog by the name of Millie. We got her from Joe Redington. She came from a top driver from the interior of Alaska. She was Nettie's leader. She was a little dog with a big heart. We purchased her as a point dog but she ended up being a great little leader. In Alaska she ran on an unlimited team. On one occasion, Nettie was ahead and I caught up with her. She had Millie in lead and I gave a command. I have often said it was the McCrum Road surge and Millie was determined to stay with me. We passed several teams. Millie couldn't keep up the pace so I went out of sight. Then the teams that we went by, passed Nettie.

Frosty

After crossing the finish line and at the truck, Millie rolled in the snow—a happy little dog along with a happy Nettie after working so hard to keep up with me. I think I won the race. That was one of my good years.

Another dog comes to mind that we got from Martin Buser. She was a young back-up dog for Martin's second Iditarod team. She was less than 2 years old and already had over a thousand miles under her feet. Nettie wanted a special dog so we got her one from Martin. Her name was Biko. We got a litter of pups from her that turned out pretty well.

Over the years we've had some pretty good dogs. Of course, some were better than others. But it's an endless job of wanting to come up with better dogs all the time. You need to do this in order to better yourself.

We had a little female called Jill. It was a delight to have her in front of the team. I almost never had to give her a command. She somehow knew which way we were to go. I guess you call this mental telepathy.

Some Special Snowshoes (7ft.) I made on special request–just for show in a museum (The Whitetail Museum in Jackson, Michigan) They have a special display of many of my things.

I have competed in races in a lot of states-Michigan, Minnesota, Montana, New York, New Hampshire, and Ontario. I've won a few and lost quite a few. I did my best in every one. Over the years, I ran with the world's best mushers.

I got started with dogs quite young but the sport of sled dog racing didn't come until the early 1960s when I was approaching 40 years old. By this time, I wasn't a teenager anymore but I did quite well in a few years, even at that age. The goal in those days was running the unlimited class. My favorite sized team was 12-14 dogs. That is why I love the sight of the big teams. They bring back a lot of memories of most of the dogs that ran in our teams over the years.

If you want to be competitive, you've got to constantly want to do better. To do better, you've got to keep getting better dogs either breeding your best to your best and picking up a good dog when you can. Of course, the best dogs generally aren't available. You've got to go to a musher who's doing well to get better bloodlines. Once in a while you can pick up a dog that can help you. Keeping on good terms with the top mushers can help.

Of late, the cross breeds that are great are German Shorthair Pointers. They are really burning up the trails so naturally most mushers are trying to have or get on a breeding program with someone. We've been lucky buying young dogs with top genes so that's improved our kennel. Once in a while you can pick up a good dog that another musher can't seem to get performance with. Not everybody is a good dog trainer and/or give up too easily. Putting a new dog in their team isn't like putting your spare tire on your car and then expecting that new dog to perform like your spare tire. A new dog needs to get used to you and the dogs they're running beside. There is more to it than meets the eye.

A lot of drivers get a dog that's a natural. He runs great for a while and then starts doing things wrong. He didn't learn anything so he has nothing to forget. I like a slow learner. He has more to remember. Once he makes your team, he's going to be there for awhile. Sometimes the best dog in your team is the most neglected. He has no problems so you spend more time paying attention to the other dogs. Dogs like to be told they are doing a good job. A young person in the sport getting started is satisfied getting all the dogs going all in the same direction at the same time. This is a comment I use once in a while. My first trip to New England, I got a charge out of several people's comments about their team. They said their team had a few good dogs but several counterfeits!

Going to some of the training that I have learned over the years, there's no substitute for training tough. So many mushers start in the fall by going as fast as the team can go. In my thoughts, that is a big mistake. I've found that by training slow and let the dog pull something slower with a little weight, muscle up the dogs first and as they muscle up then increase the speed after a month or so. The dog is less likely to get injured later. As I said before, after the dog gets tough, you can start training tough. I mean toughen those guys up. Make them pull something as they get tougher and get in condition, the faster they are going to go. Train in all kinds of sour conditions.

We've always trained with the idea of 60 degree temperature being top. That, plus humidity, shouldn't be more than 120 degrees. High humidity can be a big problem. Another thing, if it's quite cold and no snow, be sure to let the dogs have lots of liquids because in freeze dry conditions, the dogs are as thirsty as on a warm, sunny day.

A lead dog training technique that works if you want to try a new way is to train at night with a good headlight. When you come to a decision, give the dog the command and point the light in the direction you want him to go. It works. You show him the way with the headlight. Try it. It might work for you.

Another technique that keeps a dog on the side you want him to stay on is like a yoke. Oxen have been trained this way since biblical times. You take a stick like from an old broom handle about 30 inches long, fasten it in the middle to the main gangline. At either end put a snap and snap this to the dogs' collars. The dog can't go under or over the gangline to the wrong side. It works. It's like a yoke and he can't cross the line. Three or four lessons and you won't have the problem!

In hooking a dog in the gangline, be sure to snap the neckline first. Should you snap the tug first, a spooky dog can turn around and come out of the harness like taking a tee shirt off and he's gone. You don't need this problem just as you are ready to go into the starting chute. Most mushers know this but sometimes the people wanting to help hook up your dogs don't know. It's a good thing to tell them ahead of time.

The picture I love is the sight of a snowy winter trail with snow on the trees. What a beautiful sight and a good working dog team in the foreground ahead of the sled. It's a sight that nobody can take away from you. Right now I might quote part of a Robert Service poem and why I do like this picture, "It's only because of a burning love that's buried deep inside."

A day hardly goes by that the word dog isn't spoken, such as dog tired, dog dirty, dog fight, doggy bag, dog house, dog leg, dog paddle, dog tag, dog sled, dog wood, etc.

When dogs meet, they must have some kind of communication that we don't understand. I think I've solved the mystery and I have put it into a poem.

> The dogs all called a meeting
> They came from near and far.
> Some came by horse and buggy,
> While others came by car.
> Before the dogs all went inside
> And to have look
> They all took off their bung hole
> And hung it on a hook.
> Hardly had they seated
> By mother, son, and sire
> When some dirty yellow pup
> Began holler fire.
> The dogs all left in such a hurry,
> They didn't take time to look
> They just grabbed any old bung hole
> Off the bung hole hook.
> And that's the reason to this day
> That dogs upon the street
> Will sniff each other's bung
> Of every dog they meet.

So there's your answer!!

HUNTING

Hunting has been a big part of my life from early on. Sitting and listening to hunting stories by old timers was music to my young ears. My early recollection of hunting was when I just got up off the floor in Kentucky. Living close to nature as we did, hunting and guns became a common topic. Early on squirrels and rabbits-and an opossum now and then were my big game. My uncle and my second cousins were always carrying a gun somewhere.

Beef in those days was fresh killed and eaten because refrigeration was only in the future. Now pork was a different thing. You could salt it down. Every yard had a smoke house and a pile of hickory chips ready to use. I still remember smoked bacon, ham, and all the goodies: greens, beans, spinach. But squirrel and rabbit were the most common wildlife varieties. A squirrel and rabbit meant meat from the hunter's gun—in season or out.

My first gun was given to me by my grandfather. It was a single shot 410. I still have it. I shot a lot of game with it and of course missed a lot, too. Squirrels were easy but a running rabbit was different.

Then we ended up in Michigan and the hunting trend kept growing. Deer were pretty scarce in the early days. Sitting around in the evenings, listening to hunting stories, was music to my ears—stories that is from old hunters. I remember getting two rabbits in one day and of course the first time I shot a 12 gauge, and I got the rabbit, I was on my way to being a real Daniel Boone!

Even though deer were scarce in those early days, they were talked about as big game by the hunters that I listened to. A deer season finally came about where we lived and my Dad bought a 30-30 model 94 carbine and we hunted where we lived. Later, when I became old enough, I shot my first deer with that rifle. I acquired a 1917 Enfield that I sporterized.

On one occasion I shot 2 deer with one shot up west of Houghton Lake. The story about 2 deer with one shot is sort of interesting. We could get buck or doe. A friend, Jack, and I were standing a few feet apart when 3 deer came down through the woods. We stopped, Each shot once and down went the 3 deer. As we walked over to where they lay, we got to thinking about what happened. I got to figuring out the story. Jack shot the one off to the side and I shot at the two standing one ahead of the other. I had shot the one in front through the neck and the bullet got the other one standing behind. So we finally figured it out. There were four of us so we all went home with deer. My brother was one of us.

*Son Matt and I hunting at our old hunting
site in northern Michigan*

Years later a group of us went north several times. The first year was 1947. We pulled a trailer and pitched a big army surplus tent. We didn't get many deer but they were sure memorial hunts. Here in Michigan, deer weren't all that plentiful until later years when they started moving south. Now there are lots of whitetails in every state.

One fall, my cousin and I went to western Wyoming antelope and mule deer hunting. You could buy a license across the counter at that time. We each got a mule deer and had a great time. I was really hooked on trying for elk by that time.

The next hunt west was with an outfitter operating in Idaho. This was my first horseback hunt with wilderness camping on the Selway River. It was really beautiful country which literally stood on end. I found out then that those old 'hills' would make an old man out of you in a hurry! My friend, Bruce, got a mountain goat but I didn't see or get an elk. But it was a start.

My next hunt was to British Columbia. I got a black bear and hunted for 14 days with my nephew.

I played in hard luck with elk and went on three guided hunts and never saw an elk. It was great fun on horseback in the mountains. I had great fun but got no elk.

I finally booked a hunt in southwest Colorado with no guide. Up in the mountain from base camp is what we call a spike camp. I got a spike elk the first morning- hunting alone. I was hooked by that time.

Over the years I've hunted in several western states including Alaska for moose. The hunt in Alaska was a disaster. On the phone this guy sounded like a mouthy Daniel Boone. He said he had shot a moose with black powder that had an 80" spread of antlers, which borderlines records. He picked me up at the Soldotna airport in the boondocks. He said he lived in a cabin he built in seven days. I should have woke up then. He had a working wife and three small boys and a yard full of sled dogs with a lot of pups running around the yard and inside the cabin. The cabin was a one room affair. You had to duck your head to go through the door and step over a 12" log as a threshold which made the doors about 48" tall. I had scheduled three weeks with this guy.

On the way from the airport I wanted to know were he had shot the big moose so he pointed out in the bush from a dirt road going to the cabin. In two weeks he showed me three different locations he got the moose. I wanted to see the antlers and in reply was "I never bring them out of the woods." His father-in-law was a pilot who flew across the Cook Inlet to set up the camp to hunt moose. We had bought supplies so we landed and set up camp. The land there was at sea level with no hills for miles around and with brush about 10 feet tall.

Every morning, after 2 pots of coffee, he says, "Now, where shall we hunt today?"

By this time all the critters are bedded down for the day. He was the laziest man I'd ever met. After the second day he'd say, "If we don't succeed this year, we can do something different next year." It rained a lot and where we walked, the next day our tracks would be stamped out by huge bear tracks. He hunted in his sneakers. While it was raining, he hung his sneakers and muzzle loader in a small tree outside the tent-in the rain. All this was far from what I had in mind for a hunt in Alaska.

His father-in-law, the pilot, one day pulled a wrinkled note from his pocket a message from Nettie back home that her mother had stroke in Florida and had passed away. Her mother was flown to Michigan for the funeral. All this happened while I'm trying to have some fun in Alaska!

A week short of the stay I decided that was it! I got back to Anchorage airport and the only seats left on a DC10 were standby first class. Finally things started looking up. The only shot I fired on the trip was at a wolf. I missed and never saw a moose. I'd had some sour trips hunting but this one took the cake! Of course, I never went back.

One of the more exciting hunts I was on, another friend and I were up in a spike camp 12,500 feet up—where the eagles soar!. We saw a lot of elk but a bad snow storm came in and we were stranded up there for 4 ½ days. We ended up getting rescued by helicopter—dropping us down to base camp at 10,000 feet. This was an experience to remember and tell about. I still get a little nervous when it starts to snow while I am hunting.

Stranded in snow at 12,500 ft. in Oct, 1980

A couple times in Montana, with nephew Mike, I ended up in the hospital for a few days. I had quite a time trying to get a few wall hangers. I ended up with elk, antelope, mule deer, two bears, and finally a good sized whitetail full mount in the living room.

A memorial trip was in western Colorado with neighbor Bill and 2 other fellows. We packed up the mountain on horseback. Bill said to the wrangler that he wanted a slow, easy handling horse so that's what he got. By the time we got to the campsite, Bill and his horse were trailing almost a half mile. So Bill got what he wanted. The outfitter would check on us every day. The second day, Bill asked the outfitter, "How's my horse?"

The answer was, "He died last night!" When Bill got home, he found a bumper sticker that read, 'It's pretty lonesome in the saddle since my horse died.' That was pretty funny.

Bill shot his first elk on that trip. All three of us heard the slot and all were there in a few minutes. It was an event!

Several of my mule deer and antelope heads were shot with a good friend who lived north of Pontiac, Michigan. It's sometime hard to find a person that has the time and funds to go on a hunting trip. You build a relationship after a few trips together-be compatible, etc. Poor relationships can ruin a trip, a friendship, and a hunt. This fellow and I had a good thing going. We enjoyed several trips together. We did a lot of horseback trips from ranches especially in Wyoming. We had an agreement-either afoot or on horseback when we were close together. We took turns on who shot first-this with him was never broken. I remember on one occasion on horseback, just at sunset, we were in the foothills. We jumped a fair to medley buck. We both jumped off our horses and pulled our rifles out of the scab boards. I was down on one knee with rifle ready. I was waiting for him to shoot since it was his turn. He says, "What are you waiting for?"

It was a fairly long shot—300 yards or so. I made a good hit and down he went! It's good to have an agreement like that. I really thought it was his turn to shoot.

This fellow, Bruce Eavenson, and me on one of our hunts.

I've gone with other guys that an agreement meant nothing. They were just trigger happy—which made for an unhappy hunt. One trip was all you made with them.

I don't have to shoot something to have fun. Just being outdoors with mother nature and a good buddy is all it takes. If a good shot is made, you congratulate the person. That is part of being a good sportsman.

Some of my later year hunting–especially here in Michigan was with good neighbor Bill. We hunted locally on our own property and most often did quite well. Bill wanted me to hunt with him in the UP of Michigan. He had been hunting from the same old log cabin for many years. This was wilderness hunting. Not many were around pushing deer your way. Some years were pretty slow. Having an oil heated cabin after a cold wet day was great.

Bill always did the cooking and did a great job. Cabin rules said Bill didn't carry water from the well and he didn't do dishes. I hunted with Bill up there for 15-18 years. Every year was great with hunting stories, etc. We kept track of each other by walkie-talkies. We had made blinds in different locations. One year I heard Bill shoot and he said it was a big 10 point. The wind was blowing so hard that they closed the Big Mac bridge and in the woods, dead trees were falling. You'd hear them snap and made sure you'd get out of the way of where they fell! Anyway, Joe Sattler and his cousin were with us. We started trying to follow a blood trail. Bill wanted to give up as it went a certain direction and was lost.

"Well," I said, "we'll follow the blood trail and put out orange markers where we find blood." We then started looking at orange markers and that buck made a U turn and went back the direction it came from—opposite the way that Bill thought. Anyway, Joe and I followed blood and finally found the deer. It had about 8 inch spikes instead of being a 10 point. We put its head in a big clump of grass and waited for Bill to come up and see his deer.

He looked and said, "What'd I do? Shoot a doe!" It was a big laugh. Things like that made for good hunting tales.

Bill's knees gave out and had to be replaced so he didn't walk around the woods very much after that. He'd get in his pickup and drive out toward the road and sit in a blind that was easy to walk to. For years, out of that blind, Bill would have for company a big snowshoe rabbit. He'd see him several times a season. We really had a great time hunting up there. One year we celebrated the 50th year that Bill had hunted from that cabin. I'm glad I could be part of it.

Bill was about 6 years older than me and very much like an older brother. He was also a gunsmith. He worked on a lot of guns for me. My pride and joy was a gun he made from a 98 German Mauser action into a 25-06. It was a masterpiece! He made a lot of guns with the 98 action into several calibers. He got a good price for them and was always busy making one for somebody.

There are people in a lifetime that you become great friends with and if you weren't around them quite often, you felt like you were missing something. To me, Bill was that kind of a man.

When Bill died a couple years ago, I lost a true friend. There was no one to take his place in my life. On the phone, at least once a week, we'd trade tales about guns, magazines, articles, deer or turkeys we had seen out back. We always had something to talk about. When I was in his shop and seeing his work, I would have awe and whenever he stopped by in my shop, he'd do the same thing with my sled making. We were both artists—only in a different way.

Bill Rodgers, one of my true friends.

I encountered a couple grizzles—one in British Columbia in Canada and one in Montana. The one in Montana I was on horseback with a painfully pulled ham string. I had used a 7mm magnum for years. After that encounter, that gun just wasn't big enough. When I got home, I ordered a 338mag figuring if I ever went back to Alaska, I'd have rifle enough. But I never booked another hunting trip to Alaska. I did get a black bear in British Columbia and later one in Idaho.

The laws changed in Michigan to where we could hunt from an elevated stand. So I put up a tower on the southern part of my 40 acres. It was deluxe—25 feet up with sliding windows and carpeted. It was great! South of it I had a pond dug and this helps the wild critters also.

My deluxe hunting blind and my hunting tower

I had always played in bad luck getting a good, big whitetail deer. The first year though when the tower was up, a pretty good one came along and I got him with a 12 gauge slug. We can't use rifles in southern Michigan. It took me 60 years to get one his size. I had it mounted full size. He's standing in my living room even as I write this watching me.

On one of trips to the Iditarod, a furrier was on 4th Ave in Anchorage selling pelts and garments of different things. He had several big wolf pelts. One was almost black and I had to have him! The furrier figured he weighed live weight about 150 lbs. So I brought him home, the pelt that is, and had a taxidermist make it into a full mount. He's my pride and joy! I named him 'Awesome' which he is!

My Wolf "Awesome" along with some of the other wall hangers I have.

Riding our horse Misty to get ready to hunt on horseback.

Going out by horseback to a good hunting spot.

Enjoying the beautiful western countryside

Nettie's favorite picture of me hunting

Tim Karasek, my true soul mate

I want to thank you for going on this trip with me. You jumped in the sled when we started. We even traded places a couple times. You drove the team and I rode in the sled. I hope I didn't bore you with all my talk. You're a great listener. I hope I wasn't too boring. I thought we had a great time! Maybe you'll be a dog musher. As I said, you gave me someone to talk to. I want to thank you for your attention.

MY FAVORITE SAYINGS

I'm not just in the sport, I feel I'm part of the sport.

Don't stop paddling your canoe waiting for your ship to come in.

I work hard when I work, I play hard when I play, and I rest hard when I rest!

In life, a man must learn to see, not merely look.

Find something you like to do and figure out a way to get paid to do it.

Too many people work at a job they don't like, to pay for something they don't want or need. Just to keep up with other people.

A creative mess is better than idle neatness!

There are 3 kinds of people:
1. Those who make things happen.
2. Those who watch things happen.
3. Those who wonder what happened.

Find your talents and pursue your dreams.

You've got to know the ropes before you can pull the strings.

May your life be as a snowflake-leave a mark but not a stain.

A man never starts getting old until he starts to forget his dreams.

I don't like to be around a person going their way spreading the Gospel of bitterness.

It doesn't take a very big person to carry a grudge.

The best sermons are lived, not preached.

You can't be hurt by words you don't say.

Never kick a man when he's down for you don't know how big he is until he stands up.

Once I thought I was wrong, but I was mistaken.

Seeing the countryside is great but it is greater seeing it over the back of a dog team or from horseback.

The Michigan Cross Country of '73

By Frank Howard Hall

Back in the summer of '73
A great idea came to we,
As a group of dog mushers in a winter sport,
And have the North Kent club as our escort.

Seventy-five miles we had planned for this jaunt
And hoped that the tug lines would all stay taunt.
Everyone that ran that trail of white
Had to carry enough gear to camp out that night.

Late in the year that day had arrived,
The mushers all busy as bees in a hive.
The race marshall Nixon was hurrying about
To do a good job, with nothing left out.

The gang who called this meeting
Had come from near and far.
Some came by truck and camper
While others came by car.

The Thirty-seven highway
And townhall road was the site.
The dogs and gear were double checked
To make sure things were right.

Blond Pierre was first to leave;
Then Jan was close behind.
The third was Frank with a new sled
Equipped with snowhook and snub line.

Then Beckman, Harris and Nettie Hall,
Dick West and Jim Bicknell,
Montgomery, Sickles and Bob White too,
Mickivicuis, Raabe and then George Brew.

Debbie Bicknell, Murphy and Collins,
Ted Okerstrum and McCaslin finished the column.
Our feet on the sled, and pumping and running;
By keeping this pace, the camp site was coming.

Our plan was to run the old horse trail
With markers of blue that at times were pale.
The white snow came down without any gale,
Which covered all signs from beneath the tail.

The Kalkaska clubhouse was where we gather 'round
It was located at the southwest of town.
Two teams decided to camp short of the goal
As they were geared and prepared for the cold.

Thirty-six miles started fourteen and five,
Except old Frank who went fifty-five.
With the dogs all picketed and well fed,
Our camps all set up with well made beds.

That evening was spent at the sno-packers club,
The smoke and the noise like a big city pub.
A hot venison stew awaited us souls,
And as we ate, our day's stories told.

The Irish kid Murphy made himself handy,
By milling around, sharing his brandy.
The hour got late so all went to bed,
The cold made us cover from feet to our head.

Sunday dawned cold in our neat little tents,
But after we stirred, all goose bumps went.
After a big breakfast that was served by the crew
The very same ones who had served us our stew.

Then the dogs were cared for in haste and in the noise
For it wouldn't be long before, "Let's go, Boys".
So out of the town a caravan strange.
We were all headed east toward the Ausable range.

Most of the teams kept up a good pace,
But going down those hills was a white-knuckled race.
Some of the entries decided not to run
But afterwards were sorry to have missed all the fun.

Three counties this long trail did cross
With Ernie leading as our machine trail boss.
It all added up as a musher's delight,
The trail was great and the sun was out bright.

The route was safe without any dread
For our machine escorts scouted ahead.
There was Dave, Jon, Frank and Harvey too.
Jack, Bill and Jim, just to name a few.

And there at the finish the timers were waiting,
Mary, Jean and Doris stood quaking.
When all of a sudden the lead team was sighted
As a crowd had gathered with excitement delighted.

The teams crossed the finish without any band,
But the times were recorded by Doris' left hand.
Thirty-nine miles had been covered that day,
For most teams it was work and not much play.

The teams were pretty tired from first to the last
For they had worked hard to move the sled fast.
In two days they had gone seventy-five miles,
So when the finish was crossed the drivers were all smiles.

The creation of these dogs was an act of God,
Their mettle has been proved on the Iditarod.
When it was all over, it was fun for all.
It had been hard work but most had a ball.

When the drivers were asked if they'd run it again
"You better believe it," they said with a grin.
When our life is ebbing and memories told with glee,
A high light for us to say, "We ran that trail in '73.

The Newberry Cross Country of '75

By Frank Howard Hall

The Newberry group for some winter fun
Wanted something different like a sled dog run.
The summer months were busy with ideas galore;
The year that soon passed was '74

That day in March had finally arrived;
All the mushers busy as bees in a hive.
The bearded race marshall whose name was Bob White;
Doing his job making sure things were right.

The starting line was in the A&P lot
And on our sleds nothing forgot.
Cool flakes flying on the wintry day;
It wouldn't be long 'til we'd be on our way.

Columbus John was first to leave
Next Henry Schafer close behind.
Sharon and Darrell with each a sled
Gear piled high and with snub lines.

Daryl McCaslin and Ted Okerstrom, too
White shepherds pulling Monsieur George Brew.
Doug Bedell and Bob Mickevicius
Two great guys to have along with us.

Then Frank Hall many years in this sport;
Started the race wearing borrowed shorts.
Don Montgomery to the chute came running
From Mio, Michigan was Damien Lunning.

Out through the town and down the track;
A lot of miles before we'd get back.
The neighbors seemed to be real far apart
As we headed north in our depart.

One of the helpers was a chap named Matt
An accident happened and a leg bone cracked.
The seagull squawked at 8 Mile Rd.
As the northbound teams passed with heavy load.

At Pine Stump Junction, we headed east,
The bumpy trail was a real beast.
The stumps were piled high with new fallen snow,
Like huge white mushrooms with an eerie glow.

Winds from Superior toward Tahquamenon made us shiver
Over Dawson Creek and the Two Hearted River.
By Betsy, Pike and Bodi Lake, too.
There were others but these were a few.

Buckeye Al was at check point two
Made himself handy with brew and stew.
His tent was pitched in a forest tall,
The first team there was dog driver Hall.

Montgomery and McCaslin checked in soon
With tired dogs in the late afternoon.
We gathered water and got the dogs fed,
Afterwards they curled up in little round beds.

We drove east through swamp and ridges
Over frozen streams with snowy bridges;
There were sunny times when skies were bright;
Then blizzard conditions and progress afright.

So on we mushed while the dogs had the power,
The scenery changed from hour to hour.
When the snowflakes blew in the winter gale,
All was covered from beneath the dog's tails.

Winter desolation took on a new view.
The only humans were other mushers and you.
In the Paradise loop, we turned around,
Then sixty miles back to Newberry town.

The Paradise loop was checkpoint three.
John and Pete were there when we
As the teams came near, the command was gee;
After the turn, some stopped for tea.

We ran the race without much dread
With CB's keeping track and with plane overhead.
They were a big help putting on this race,
Keeping track of our positions from place to place.

Bill and Sparky were all over the place;
While Dave held things down at the radio base.
A lot of persons helped with steady surveillance
While Max and Denny were grooming the trail.

Auggie and Steve on the trail with smiles,
Tacking up markers every five miles.
Russ, Pike, and Bob with Anita, too
The helpers were many, just to name a few.

As darkness approached on the single trail,
The dogs worked great over hill and dale.
The night was dark and mushing a delight;
You should try driving your team some night.

On through the darkness and at the edge of town,
Several hundred people were gathered around.
And there at the finish line some just in time,
To cheer the winner across the finish line.

Leona was there with camera in hand,
Taking great pictures of those who ran.
While drivers were unpacking their sleds and gear,
Newberry was planning for greater things next year.

Our dogs did great through the whole race,
They worked real hard and held a good pace.
These dogs are here, created by God.
Two mushers named this race the I-Did-It-Rod.

The teams came in from time to time.
Most were all smiles when they crossed the line.
Most finishers had some weird tales to tell.
The next gathering we had was at the Falls Hotel.

A banquet was in order and the attendants had a ball
Cross country patches were received by all.
The town by vote was in the Sportsman's camp
With all the team drivers being the champs.

We the drivers stand in silent salute,
Paying our respects to the Newberry group.
The mushers heading home were full of good cheer,
While Newberry was saying, "The mushers have been here."

When the years have come
And our days they pine
Our names will be written
On the MUSHER"S TRAIL OF TIME.